*Interesting Account of
Several Remarkable Visions*

By Orson Pratt

Copyright © 2021 Lamp of Trismegistus. All rights reserved. No part of this publication may be reproduced or transmitted in any form or by any means, electronic or mechanical, including photocopying, recording, or by any information storage and retrieval system, without permission in writing from Lamp of Trismegistus. Reviewers may quote brief passages.

ISBN: 978-1-63118-553-3

*Mormon History
Series*

Other Books in this Series and Related Titles

Pearl of Great Price by Joseph Smith (978-1-63118-539-7)

The Angel of the Prairies or A Dream of the Future: Mormon History Series By Elder Parley Parker Pratt (978-1-63118-541-0)

A Manuscript on Far West by Reed Peck (978-1-63118-544-1)

The Story of Mormonism by James E Talmage (978-1-63118-543-4)

An Address to All Believers in Christ Elder David Whitmer (978-1-63118-545-8)

The Philosophy of Mormonism by James E Talmage (978-1-63118-542-7)

The Book of John Whitmer by John Whitmer (978-1-63118-554-0)

The Book of Abraham: Mormon History by George Reynolds (978-1-63118-540-3)

The Testament of Abraham by Abraham (978-1-63118-441-3)

Private Diary of Joseph Smith 1832-1834 (978-1-63118-546-5)

Times and Seasons Volume 1, Numbers 1-3 (978-1-63118-555-7)

Times and Seasons Volume 1, Numbers 4-6 (978-1-63118-556-4)

The Evening and Morning Star Volume 1, Numbers 1 & 2 (978-1-63118-547-2)

The Evening and Morning Star Volume 1, Numbers 3 & 4 (978-1-63118-548-9)

The Evening and Morning Star Volume 1, Numbers 5 & 6 (978-1-63118-549-6)

The Evening and Morning Star Volume 1, Numbers 7 & 8 (978-1-63118-550-2)

The Evening and Morning Star Volume 1, Numbers 9 & 10 (978-1-63118-551-9)

The Evening and Morning Star Volume 1, Numbers 11 & 12 (978-1-63118-552-6)

The Testament of Moses by Moses (978-1-63118-440-6)

Book of Dreams by Enoch (978-1-63118-437-6)

The Book of Astronomical Secrets by Enoch (978-1-63118-443-7)

Audio versions are also available on Audible, Amazon and Apple

Other Books in this Series and Related Titles

American Indian Freemasonry by A C Parker (978-1-63118-460-4)

The Hidden Mysteries of Christianity by Annie Besant (978–1–63118–534–2)

Rosicrucian Rules, Secret Signs, Codes and Symbols by various (978-1-63118-488-8)

History and Teachings of the Rosicrucians by W W Westcott &c (978-1-63118-487-1)

Freemasonry and the Egyptian Mysteries by C. W. Leadbeater (978-1-63118-456-7)

The Sepher Yetzirah and the Qabalah by M P Hall (978-1-63118-481-9)

The Psalms of Solomon by King Solomon (978-1-63118-439-0)

The Historic, Mythic and Mystic Christ by Annie Besant (978–1–63118–533–5)

The Book of Parables by Enoch (978-1-63118-429-1)

The Secrets of Enoch by Enoch (978-1-63118-449-9)

The Book of the Watchers by Enoch (978-1-63118-416-1)

The Old Past Master by Carl H Claudy (978-1-63118-464-2)

The Influence of Pythagoras on Freemasonry and Other Essays (978-1-63118-404-8)

The Mysteries of Freemasonry & the Druids by various (978-1-63118-444-4)

Masonic Symbolism of the Apron & the Altar by various (978-1-63118-428-4)

The Book of Wisdom of Solomon by King Solomon (978-1-63118-502-1)

Masonic Symbolism of Easter and the Christ in Masonry (978-1-63118-434-5)

The Odes of Solomon by King Solomon (978-1-63118-503-8)

Ancient Mysteries and Secret Societies by M P Hall (978-1-63118-410-9)

The Golden Verses of Pythagoras: Five Translations (978-1-63118-479-6)

Freemasonry & Catholicism by Max Heindel (978-1-63118-508-3)

A Few Masonic Sermons by A. C. Ward &c (978-1-63118-435-2)

Audio versions are also available on Audible, Amazon and Apple

Table of Contents

*Interesting Account of
Several Remarkable Visions*

Title Page…7

Part I: *First Vision*…9

Part II: *Golden Plates*…13

Part III: *Book of Mormon Geography*…25

Part IV: *Three Witnesses*…37

Part V: *Church Doctrine*…41

A

INTERESTING ACCOUNT

OF

SEVERAL REMARKABLE VISIONS

AND OF

THE LATE DISCOVERY

OF

ANCIENT AMERICAN RECORDS

BY O. PRATT

MINISTER OF THE GOSPEL

"For there is nothing covered, that shall not be revealed; and hid, that shal not be known." — Matt. X. 26.

EDINBURGH:

PRINTED BY BALLANTYNE AND HUGHES,

MDCCCXL

PART I:
FIRST VISION

FACTS
IN RELATION TO THE LATE DISCOVERY OF ANCIENT AMERICAN RECORDS

Mr. Joseph Smith, jun., who made the following important discovery, was born in the town of Sharon, Windsor county, Vermont, on the 23rd of December, A.D. 1805. When ten years old, his parents, with their family, moved to Palmyra, New York; in the vicinity of which he resided for about eleven years, the latter part in the town of Manchester. Cultivating the earth for a livelihood was his occupation, in which employed the most of his time. His advantages, for acquiring literary knowledge, were exceedingly small; hence, his education was limited to a slight acquaintance with two or three of the common branches of learning. He could read without much difficulty, and write a very imperfect hand; and had a very limited understanding of the ground rules of arithmetic.

These were his highest and only attainments; while the rest of those branches, so universally taught in the common schools throughout the United States, were entirely unknown to him. When somewhere about fourteen or fifteen years old, he began seriously to reflect upon the necessity of being prepared for a future state of existence: but how, or in what way, to prepare himself, was a question, as yet, undetermined in his own mind: he perceived that it was a question of infinite importance, and that the salvation of his soul depended upon a correct understanding of the same. He saw, that if he understood not the way, it would be impossible to walk in it, except by chance; and the thought of resting his hopes of eternal life upon chance, or uncertainties, was more than he could endure.

If he went to the religious denominations to seek information, each one pointed to its particular tenants saying -- "This is the way, walk ye in it;" while at the same time, the doctrines of each were, in many respects, in direct opposition to one another.

It also occurred to his mind, that God was not the author of but one doctrine, and therefore could not acknowledge but one denomination as his church; and that such denomination must be a people who believe and teach that one doctrine, whatever it may be, and build upon the same. He then reflected upon the immense number of doctrines now in the world, which had given rise to many hundreds of different denominations. The great question to be decided in his mind was --- if any one of these denominations be the Church of Christ, which one is it? Until he could become satisfied, in relation to this question, he could not rest contented.

To trust to the decisions of fallible man, and build his hopes upon the same without any certainty and knowledge, of his own, would not satisfy the anxious desires that pervaded his breast. To decide, without any positive and definite evidence on which he could rely, upon a subject involving the future welfare of his soul, was revolting to his feelings.

The only alternative that seemed to be left his was to read the Scriptures, and endeavor to follow their directions. He, accordingly, commenced pursuing the sacred pages of the Bible, with sincerity, believing the things he read.

His mind soon caught hold of the following passage: -- "If any of you lack wisdom, let him ask of God, that giveth to all men liberally and upbraideth not; and it shall be given him." -- James i, 5.

Form this promise he learned that it was the privilege of all men to ask God for wisdom, with the sure and certain expectation of receiving, liberally, without being upbraided for so doing. This was cheering information to him: tidings that gave him great joy. It was like a light shining forth in a dark place, to guide him to the path in which he should walk.

He now saw that if he inquired of God, there was not only a possibility but a probability, yea more a certainty, that he should obtain a knowledge which of all the doctrines was the doctrine of Christ, and which of all the church was a church of Christ. He, therefore, retired to a secret place, in a grove but a short distance from his father's house, and knelt down and began to call upon the Lord.

At first he was severely tempted by the powers of darkness which endeavored to overcome him, but he continued to seek for deliverance until darkness gave way from his mind, and he was enabled to pray in fervency of the spirit and in faith. And while thus pouring out his soul, anxiously desiring an answer from God, he at length saw a very bright and glorious light in the heavens above, which at first seemed to be a considerable distance.

He continued praying while the light appeared to be gradually descending towards him; and as it drew nearer, it increased in brightness and magnitude, so that by the time it reached the tops of the trees the whole wilderness, for some distance around, was illuminated in a most glorious and brilliant manner. He expected to have seen the leaves and boughs of the trees consumed as soon as the light came in contact with them, but perceiving that it did not produce that effect, he was encouraged with the hopes of being able to endure its presence.

It continued descending, slowly, until it rested upon the earth, and he was enveloped in the midst of it. When it first came upon him, it produced a peculiar sensation throughout his whole system, and immediately his mind was caught away from the natural objects with which he was surrounded, and he was enwrapped in a heavenly vision and saw two glorious personages who exactly resembled each other in their features or likeness. He was informed that his sins were forgiven. He was also informed upon the subjects which had for some time previously agitated his mind, viz. -- that all the religious denominations were believing in incorrect doctrines; and, consequently, that none of them was acknowledged of God as his church and kingdom. And he was expressly commanded to go not after them, and he received a promise that the true doctrine -- the fullness of the gospel -- should at some future time be made known to him; after which the vision withdrew, leaving his mind in a state of calmness and peace, indescribable.

Some time after having received this glorious manifestation, being young, he was again entangled in the vanities of the world, of which he afterwards sincerely and truly repented.

PART II:
GOLDEN PLATES

And it pleased God, on the evening of the 21st of September, A.D. 1823, to again hear his prayers. For he had retired to rest, as usual, only that his mind was drawn out in fervent prayer, and his soul was filled with the most earnest desire "to commune with some kind messenger, who could communicate to him the desired information of his acceptance with God" and also unfold the principles of the doctrine of Christ, according to the promise which he had received in the former vision.

While he thus continued to pour out his desires before the Father of all good, endeavoring to exercise faith in his precious promises,

> *"on a sudden a light like that of day, only of a purer and far more glorious appearance and brightness, burst into the room. Indeed, the first sight was as though the house was filled with consuming fire. This sudden appearance of a light so bright, as must naturally be expected, occasioned a shock or sensation visible to the extremities of the body. It was, however, followed with a calmness and serenity of mind, and not overwhelming rapture of joy, that surpassed understanding, and in a moment, a personage stood before him."*

Notwithstanding the brightness of the light which previously illuminated the room,

> *"yet there seemed to be an additional glory surrounding or accompanying this personage, which shone with an increased degree of brilliancy, of which he was in the midst; and though his continence was as lightning, yet it was of a pleasing, innocent, and glorious appearance; so much so*

that every fear was banished from the hear and nothing but calmness pervaded the soul".

"The stature of this personage was a little above the common size of men in this age; his garment was perfectly white and had the appearance of being without seam."

This glorious being declared himself to be an Angel of God, sent forth by commandment, to communicate to him that his sins were forgiven and that his prayers were heard; and also to bring joyful tidings that the covenant which God made with ancient Israel, concerning their posterity, was at hand to be fulfilled; that the great preparatory work for the second coming of the Messiah was speedily to commence; that the time was at hand for the gospel, in its fullness, to be preached in power unto all nations; that a people might be prepared with faith and righteousness, for the Millennial reign of universal peace and joy.

He was informed that he was called and chosen to be an instrument in the hands of God, to bring about some of his marvelous purposes in this glorious dispensation. It was also made manifest to him that the "American Indians" were a remnant of Israel. That when they first emigrated to America they were an enlightened people, possessing a knowledge of the true God, enjoying his favor and peculiar blessings from his hand. That the prophets and inspired writers among them were required to keep a sacred history of the most important events transpiring among them. Which history was handed down for many generations, till at length they fell into great wickedness, the most part of them were destroyed, and the records (by commandment of God to one of the last prophets among them) were safely deposited, to preserve them from the hands of the wicked who sought to destroy them.

He was informed that the records contained many sacred revelations pertaining to the gospel of the kingdom as well as the prophecies relating to the great events of the last days, and that to fulfill his promises to the ancients, who wrote the records, and to accomplish his purposes in the restitution of their children, &c, they were to come forth to the knowledge of the people. If faithful, he was to be the instrument who should be thus highly favored in bringing these sacred things to light. At the same time, being expressly informed, that it must be done with an eye single to the glory of God, that no one could be entrusted with those sacred writings who should endeavor to aggrandize himself, by converting sacred things to unrighteous and speculative purposes.

After giving him many instructions concerning things past and to come, which would be foreign to our purpose to mention here, he disappeared. And the light and glory of God withdrew leaving his mind in perfect peace, while a calmness and serenity indescribable pervaded the soul. But, before morning, the vision was twice renewed, instructing him further and still further concerning the great work of God about to be performed on the earth.

In the morning he went out to his labor as usual, but soon the vision was renewed. The Angel appeared, and having been informed by the previous visions of the night concerning the place where those records were deposited, he was instructed to go immediately and view them.

Accordingly, he repaired to the place, a brief description of which shall be given, in the words of a gentleman by the name of Oliver Cowdery, who has visited the spot:

"As you pass on the mail-road from Palmyra, Wayne County, to Canandaigua, Ontario County, New York, before arriving at the little village of Manchester, say from three to four, or about four miles from Palmyra, you pass a large hill on the east side of the road. Why I say large, is because it is as large perhaps as any in that country.

"The north end rises quite suddenly until it assumes a level with the more southerly extremity, and I think I must say, an elevation higher than at the south, a short distance, say half or three-fourths of a mile. As you pass towards Canandaigua, it lessens gradually until the surface assumes its common level, or is broken by other smaller hills or ridges, water courses and ravines. I think I am justified in say that this is the highest hill for some distance around, and I am certain that its appearance, as it rises so suddenly from the plain on the north, must attract the notice of the traveler as he passes by.

"The north end," which as been described as rising suddenly from the plain, forms "a promontory without timber, but covered with grass. As you pass to the south, you soon come to scattering timber, the surface having been cleared by art or wind; and a short distance further left you are surrounded with common forest of the country. It is necessary to observe that even the part cleared was only occupied for pasturage: its steep ascent and narrow summit not admitting the plow of the husbandman with any degree of ease or profit. It was at the second mentioned place where the record was found to be deposited, on the west side of the hill, not far from the top down its side; and when myself visited the place in the year 1830, there were several trees standing -- enough to cause a shade in summer but not so much as to prevent the surface being covered with grass -- which was also the case when the record was first found.

"How far below the surface these records were (anciently) placed, I am unable to say. But from the fact that they had been some fourteen hundred years buried, and that too on the side of a hill so steep, one is ready to conclude that they were some feet below, as the earth would naturally wear more or less in that length of time. But they, being placed toward the top of the hill, the ground would not remove as much as two-thirds, perhaps.

"Another circumstance would prevent a wearing of the earth: in all probability as soon as timber had time to grow, the hill was covered and the roots of the same would hold the surface. However, on this point, I shall leave every man to draw his own conclusion and form is own speculation."

But suffice to say "a hole of sufficient depth was dug. At the bottom of this was laid a stone of suitable size, the upper surface being smooth. At each edge was placed a large quantity of cement, and into this cement, at the four edges of this stone, were placed erect four others: their bottom edges resting in the cement, at the outer edges of the first stone.

"The four last named, when placed erect, formed a box. The corners, or where the edges of the four came in contact, were also cemented so firmly that the moisture from without was prevented from entering. It is to be observed also that the inner surfaces of the four erect, or side stones, were smooth. This box was sufficiently large to admit a breastplate, such as was used by the ancients, to defend the chest, &c., from the arrows and weapons of their enemy. From the bottom of the box, or from the breastplate, arose three small pillars, composed of the same description of cement used on the edges, an upon these three pillars were placed the records.

"This box, containing the records, was covered with another stone, the bottom surface being flat, and the upper crowning." When it was first visited by Mr. Smith, on the morning of the 22nd of September 1823, *"a part of the crowning stone was visible above the surface while the edges were concealed by the soil and grass."* From which circumstance, it may be seen *"that however deep this box might have been placed at first, the time had been sufficient to wear the earth, so that it was easily discovered when once directed and yet not enough to make a perceivable difference to the passer-by.*

"After arriving at the repository, a little exertion in removing the soil from the edges of the top of the box, and a light pry, brought to his natural vision its contents." While viewing and contemplating this sacred treasure with wonder and astonishment, behold! The Angel of the Lord, who had previously visited him, again stood in his presence. And his soul was again enlightened as it was the evening before, and he was filled with the Holy Spirit. And the heavens were opened, and the glory of the Lord shone round about and rested upon him. While he thus stood gazing and admiring, the Angel said Look! And as he thus spake, he beheld the Prince of Darkness, surrounded by his innumerable train of associates. All this passed before him, and the heavenly messenger said "All this is shown, the good and the evil, the holy and impure, the glory of God, and the power of darkness, that you may now hereafter the two powers, and never be influenced or overcome by that wicked one.*

"Behold, whatsoever enticeth and leadeth to good and do good, is of God. And whatsoever doth not, is of the wicked one. It is he that filleth the hearts of men with evil, to walk in darkness and blaspheme God; and you may learn from henceforth that his ways are to destruction, but the way of holiness is peace and rest. You cannot at this time obtain this record, for the commandment of God is strict, and if ever these sacred

things are obtained, they must be by prayer and faithfulness in obeying the Lord.

"They are not deposited here for the sake of accumulating gain and wealth for the glory of this world; they were sealed by the prayer of faith, and because of the knowledge which they contain. They are of no worth among the children of men, only for their knowledge.

"On them is contained the fullness of the gospel of Jesus Christ, as it was given to his people on this land, and when it shall be brought forth by the power of God, it shall be carried to the Gentiles, of whom many will receive it, and after will the seed of Israel be brought into the fold of their Redeemer by obeying it also.

"Those who kept the commandments of the Lord on this land, desired this at his hand and through the prayer of faith obtained the promise, that if their descendants should transgress and fall away, that a record should be kept, and in the last days come ot their children.

"These things are sacred and must be kept so, for the promise of the Lord concerning them must be fulfilled. No man can obtain them if his heart is impure, because they contain that which is sacred." * * * "By them will the Lord work a great and marvelous work, the wisdom of the wise shall become as naught, and the understanding of the prudent shall be hid, and because of the power of God shall be displayed, those who profess to know the truth, but walk in deceit, shall tremble with anger; but with signs and with wonders, with gifts and with healings, with the manifestations of the power of God, and with the Holy Ghost, shall the hearts of the faithful be comforted.

"You have now beheld the power of God manifested, and the power of Satan. You see that there is nothing desirable in the works of darkness,

that they cannot bring happiness, and those who are overcome therewith are miserable. While on the other hand, the righteous are blessed with a place in the kingdom of God, where joy unspeakable surrounds them. There they rest beyond the power of the enemy of truth, where no evil can disturb them. The glory of God crowns them and they continually feast upon his goodness, and enjoy his smiles.

"Behold, notwithstanding you have seen this great display of power by which you may ever be able to detect the evil one, yet I give unto you another sign, and when it comes to pass then know that the Lord is God, and that he will fulfill his purposes, and that the knowledge which this record contains will go to every nation, and kindred, and tongue, and people under the whole heaven.

"This is the sign: when these things begin to be known, that is, when it is known that the Lord has shown you these things, the workers of iniquity will seek to overthrow. They will circulate falsehoods to destroy your reputation and also will seek to take your life. But remember this: if you are faithful and shall hereafter continue to keep the commandments of the Lord, you shall be preserved to bring these things forth, for in due time he will give you a commandment to come and take them.

"When they are interpreted, the Lord will give the hold priesthood to some, and they shall begin to proclaim this gospel and baptize by water. And after that they shall have power to give the Holy Ghost by the laying on of their hands. Then will persecution rage more and more; for the iniquities of men shall be revealed. And those who are not built upon the Rock will seek to overthrow the church. But it will increase the more opposed and spread farther and farther, increasing in knowledge till they shall be sanctified and receive an inheritance where the glory of God will rest upon them. And when this takes place, and all things are prepared,

the ten tribes of Israel will be revealed in the north country, whither they have been for a long season, and when this is fulfilled will be brought to pass that saying of the prophet 'And the Redeemer shall come to Zion, and unto them that turn from transgression in Jacob, saith the Lord.' But notwithstanding the workers of iniquity shall seek your destruction, the arm of the Lord will be extended and you will be borne off conqueror if you keep all his commandments.

"Your name shall be known among the nations, for the work which the Lord will perform by your hands shall cause the righteous to rejoice and the wicked to rage; with the one it shall be had in honor, and with the other in reproach; yet with these it shall be a terror, because of the great and marvelous work which shall follow the coming forth of this fullness of the gospel. Now, go they way, remembering what the Lord has done for thee, and be diligent in keeping his commandments, and he will deliver thee from temptations and all the arts and devices of the wicked one. Forget not to pray, that thy mind may become strong, that when he shall manifest unto thee, thou mayest have power to escape the evil and obtain these precious things."

We here remark that the above quotation is an extract from a letter written by Elder Oliver Cowdery, which was published in one of the numbers of the "Latter Day Saints' Messenger and Advocate".

Although many more instructions were given by the mouth of the angel to Mr. Smith, which we do not write in this book, yet most of the important items are contained in the foregoing relation. During the period of the four following years, he frequently received instruction from the mouth of the heavenly messenger. And on the morning of the 22nd of September, A.D. 1827, the angel of the Lord delivered the records into his hands.

These records were engraved on plates, which had the appearance of gold. Each plate was not far from seven by eight inches in width and length, being not quite as thick as common tin. They were filled on both sides with engravings, in Egyptian characters, and bound together in a volume, as the leaves of a book, and fastened at one edge with three rings running through the whole. This volume was something near six inches in thickness, a part of which was sealed. The characters or letters upon the unsealed part were small and beautifully engraved. The whole book exhibited many marks of antiquity in its construction, as well as much skill in the art of engraving.

With the records was found "a curious instrument, called by the ancients the Urim and Thummim, which consisted of two transparent stones, clear as crystal, set in the two rimes of a bow. This was in use, in ancient times, by persons called seers. It was an instrument by the use of which they received revelation of things distant or of things past or future."

In the mean time, the inhabitants of that vicinity, have been informed that Mr. Smith had seen heavenly visions, and that he had discovered sacred records, began to ridicule and mock at those things. And after having obtained those sacred things, while proceeding home through the wilderness and fields, he was waylaid by two ruffians who had secreted themselves for the purpose of robbing him of the records.

One of them struck him with a club before he perceived them, but the other being a strong man and large in stature, with great exertion he cleared himself from them and ran towards home, being closely pursued until he came near his father's house, when his pursuers, for fear of being detected, turned and fled the other way.

Soon the news of is discoveries spread abroad throughout all of those parts. False reports, misrepresentations, and base slanders flew as if upon the wings of the wind in every direction. The house was frequently beset by mobs and evil designing persons. Several times he was shot at, and very narrowly escaped. Every device was used to get the plates away from him. And being continually in danger of his life, from a gang of abandoned wretches, he at length concluded to leave the place and go to Pennsylvania, and accordingly packed up his goods, putting the plates into a barrel of beans, and proceeded upon his journey.

He had not gone far, before he was overtaken by an officer with a search warrant, who flattered himself with the idea that he should surely obtain the plates. After searching very diligently, he was sadly disappointed at not finding them. Mr. Smith then drove on, but before he got to his journey's end he was again overtaken by an officer on the same business, and after ransacking the wagon very carefully, he went his way as much chagrined as the first, at not being able to discover the object of his research. Without any further molestation, he pursued his journey until he came into the northern part of Pennsylvania, near the Susquehannah river, in which part his father-in-law resided.

Having provided himself with a home, he commenced translating the record, by the gift and power of God, through the means of the Urim and Thummim. And being a poor writer, he was under the necessity of employing a scribe, to write the translation as it came from his mouth.

PART III:
BOOK OF MORMON GEOGRAPHY

In the mean time, a few of the original characters were accurately transcribed and translated by Mr. Smith, which with the translation, were taken by a gentleman by the name of Martin Harris to New York, where they wer presented to a learned gentleman by the name of Anthon, who professed to be extensively acquainted with many languages, both ancient and modern. He examined them, but was unable to decipher them correctly. But he presumed that if the original records could be brought, he could assist in translating them.

But to return, Mr. Smith continued the work of the translation, as his pecuniary circumstances would permit, until he finished the unsealed part of the records. The part translated is entitled the "Book of Mormon", which contains nearly as much reading as the Old Testament.

In this important and most interesting book, we can read the history of Ancient America, from its early settlement by a colony who cam from the tower of Babel, at the confusion of languages, to the beginning of the fifth century of the Christian era. By these Records we are informed that America, in ancient times, has been inhabited by two distinct races of people. The first, or more ancient race, came directly from the great tower, being called Jaredites. The second race came directly from the city of Jerusalem, about six hundred years before Christ, being Israelites, principally the descendants of Joseph.

The first nation, or Jaredites, were destroyed about the time that the Israelites came from Jerusalem, who succeeded them in the inheritance of the country. The principle nation of the second race fell in battle towards the close of the fourth century. The remaining remnant, having dwindled into an uncivilized state, still continue to inhabit the land, although divided into a "multitude of nations" and are called by Europeans as the "American Indians."

We learn from this very ancient history that at the confusion of languages, when the Lord scattered the people upon all the face of the earth, the Jaredites, being a righteous people, obtained favour in the sight of the Lord and were not confounded. And because of their righteousness, the Lord miraculously led them from the tower to the great ocean, where they were commanded to build vessels, in which they were marvelously brought across the great deep to the shores of North America.

And the Lord God promised to give them America, which was a very choice land in his sight, for an inheritance. And He swore unto them in his wrath, that whoso should possess this land of promise, from the time henceforth and forever, should serve him, the true and only God, or they should be swept off when the fullness of his wrath should come upon them and they were fully ripened in iniquity. Moreover, he promised to make them a great and powerful nation, so that there should be no greater nation upon all the face of the earth.

Accordingly, in process of time, they became a very numerous and powerful people, occupying principally North America, building large cities in all quarters of the land, (and) being a civilized and enlightened nation. Agriculture and machinery were carried on to a great extent. Commercial and manufacturing business flourished on every hand, yet in consequence of wickedness, they were often visited with terrible judgments. Many prophets were raised up among them from generation to generation, who testified against the wickedness of the people and prophesied of judgments and calamities which awaited them, if they did not repent.

Sometimes they were visited by pestilence and plagues, and sometimes by famine and war, until at length (having occupied the land some fifteen or sixteen hundred years) their wickedness became so great that the Lord threatened, by the mouth of his prophets, to utterly destroy them from the face of the land. But they gave no heed to these warnings, therefore the word of the Lord was fulfilled and they were entirely destroyed leaving their houses, their cities, and their land desolate. And their sacred records also, which were kept on gold plates, were left by one of their last prophets whose name was Ether, in such a situation that they were discovered by the remnant of Joseph, who soon afterwards were brought from Jerusalem to inherit the land.

This remnant of Joseph were also led in miraculous manner from Jerusalem, in the first year of the reign of Zedekiah, king of Judah. They were first led to the eastern borders of the Red Sea, then they journeyed for some time along the borders thereof, nearly in a south-east direction, after which they altered their course nearly eastward until they came to the great waters where, by the commandment of God, they built a vessel in which they were safely brought across the great Pacific Ocean and landed upon the western coast of South America.

In the eleventh year of the reign of Zedekiah, at the time the Jews were carried away captive into Babylon, another remant were brought out of Jerusalem, some of whom were descendants of Judah. They landed in North America, soon after which they emigrated into the northern parts of South America, at which place they were discovered by the remnant of Joseph, something like four hundred years after.

From these ancient records, we learn that this remnant of Joseph, soon after they landed, separated themselves into two distinct nations. This division was caused by certain portion of them being greatly persecuted because of their righteousness, by the remainder. The persecuted nation emigrated towards the north parts of South America, leaving the wicked nation in possession of the middle and southern parts of the same.

The former were called Nephites, being led by a prophet whose name was Nephi. The latter were called Lamanites, being led by a very wicked man whose name was Laman. The Nephites had in their possession a copy of the Hold Scriptures, viz. the five books of Moses, and the prophecies of the holy prophets down to Jeremiah, in whose days they left Jerusalem.

These Scriptures were engraved on plates of brass, in the Egyptian language. They themselves also made plates, soon after landing, on which they began to engrave their own history, prophecies, visions, and revelations. All these sacred records were kept by holy and righteous men, who were inspired by the Holy Ghost, and were carefully preserved and handed down from generation to generation.

And the Lord gave unto them the whole continent, for a land of promise, and he promised that they, and their children after them, should inherit it on condition of their obedience to his commandments. But if they were disobedient, they should be cut off from his presence.

And the Nephites began to prosper in the land, according to their righteousness, and they multiplied and spread forth to the east, and west, and north; building large villages and cities, synagogues and temples, together with forts and towers and fortifications, to defend themselves against their enemies.

And they cultivated the earth and raised various kinds of grain in abundance. They also raised numerous flocks of domestic animals and became a very wealthy people, having abundance gold, silver, copper, tin, iron, &c. Arts and sciences flourished to a great extent. Various kinds of machinery were in use. Cloths of various kinds were manufactured. Swords, scimitars, axes, and various implements of war were made, together with head shields, arm shields, and breastplates, to defend themselves in battle with their enemies. And in the days of their righteousness, they were a civilized, enlightened, and happy people.

But on the other hand, the Lamanites, because of the hardness of their hearts, brought down many judgments upon their own heads. Nevertheless, they were not destroyed as a nation, but the Lord God sent forth a curse upon them, and they became a dark, loathsome, and filthy people. Before their rebellion, they were white and exceedingly fair, like the Nephites, but the Lord God cursed them in their complexions, and they were changed to a dark color, and they became a wild, savage, and ferocious people, being great enemies to the Nephites, whom they south by every means to destroy. And many times came against them, with their numerous hosts to battle, but were repulsed by the Nephites and driven back to their own possessions, not however generally speaking without great loss on both sides. For tends of thousands were very frequently slain, after which they were piled together in great heaps upon the face of the ground and covered with a shallow covering of earth, which will satisfactorily account for those ancient mounds, filled with human bones, so numerous at the present day both in North and South America.

The second colony, which left Jerusalem eleven years after the remnant of Joseph left that city, landed in North America and emigrated from thence, to the north pars of South America; and about four hundred years after they were discovered by the Nephites, as we stated in the foregoing.

They were called the people of Zarahemla. They had been perplexed with many wars among themselves, and having brought no records with them, their language had become corrupted and they denied the being of God. And at the time they were discovered by the Nephites they were very numerous, and only in a partial state of civilization. But the Nephites united with them and taught them the Holy Scriptures, and they were restored to civilization and became one nation with them.

And And in process of time, the Nephites began to build ships near the Isthmus of Darien, and launch them forth into the western ocean, in which great numbers ailed a great distance to the northward and began to colonize North America. Other colonies emigrated by land and in a few centuries the whole continent became peopled. North America, at that time, was almost entirely destitute of timber, it having been cut off by the more ancient race, who came from the great tower at the confusion of languages, but the Nephites became very skillful in building houses of cement. Also, much timber was carried by way of shipping from South to North America.

They also planted groves and began to raise timber, that in time their wants might be supplied. Large cities were built in various parts of the continent, both among the Lamanites and Nephites. The law of Moses was observed by the latter. Numerous prophets were raised up from time to time throughout their generations.

Many records, both historical and prophetical, which were of great size, were kept among them. Some on plates of gold and other metals, and some on other materials. The sacred records, also of the more ancient race who at been destroyed, were found by them. These were engraved on plates of gold. They translated them into their own language by the gift and power of God, through the means of the Urim and Thummim. They contained an historical account from the creation down to the Tower of Babel, and from that time down until they were destroyed, comprising a period of about thirty-four hundred or thirty-five hundred years. They also contained many prophecies, great and marvelous, reaching forward to the final end and consummation of all things, and the creation of the new heaven and new earth.

The prophets also among the Nephites prophesied of great things. They opened the secrets of futurity, and saw the coming of Messiah in the flesh, and prophesied of the blessings to come upon their descendants in the latter times. And made known the history of unborn generations and unfolded the grand events of ages to come. And viewed the power and glory and majesty of Messiah's second advent. And beheld the establishment of the kingdom of peace and gazed upon the glories of the day of righteousness and saw the creation redeemed from the curse, and all the righteous filled with songs of everlasting joy.

The Nephites knew of the birth and crucifixion of Christ, by certain celestial and terrestrial phenomena, which at time time were shown forth in fulfillment of the predictions of many of their prophets. Notwithstanding the many blessings with which they had been blessed, they had fallen into great wickedness and had cast out the saints and the prophets, and stoned and killed them.

Therefore, at the time of the crucifixion of Christ, they were visited in great judgment. Thick darkness covered the whole continent. The earth was terribly convulsed. The rocks were rent into broken fragments and afterwards found in seams and cracks upon all the face of the land. Mountains were sunk into valleys, and valleys raised into mountains. The highways and level roads were broken up and spoiled. Many cities were laid in ruins. Others were buried up in the depths of the earth and mountains occupied their place. While others were sunk and the waters came up in their stead, and other still were burned by fire from heaven.

Thus, the predictions of their prophets were fulfilled upon their heads. Thus the more wicket part, both of the Nephites and Lamanites, were destroyed. Thus, the Almighty executed vengeance and fury upon them that the blood of the saints and prophets might no longer cry from the ground against them.

Those who survived these terrible judgments were favored with the personal ministry of Christ. For after He arose from the dead and finished his ministry at Jerusalem, and ascended to heaven, he descended in the presence of the Nephites, who were assembled round about their temples in the northern pars of South America. He exhibited to them his wounded hands and side and feet, and commanded the law of Moses to be abolished, and introduced and established the Gospel in its stead. And chose twelve disciples from among them to administer the same, and instituted the sacrament, and prayed for and blessed their little children. And healed their sick, and blind, and lame, and deaf, and those who were afflicted in any way. And raised a man from the dead and showed forth his power in their midst. And expounded the Scriptures, which had been given from the beginning down to that time, and made known unto them all things which should take place down until He should come in his glory, and form that time down to the end, when all people, nations, and languages should stand before God to be judged, and the heaven and the earth should pass away and there should be a new heaven and new earth. These teachings of Jesus were engraved upon plates, some of which are contained in the book of Mormon, but the more part are not revealed in that book, but are hereafter to be made manifest to the saints.

After Jesus had finished ministering unto them, he ascended into heaven. And the twelve disciples, who he had chosen, went forth upon all the face of the land, preaching the gospel, baptizing those who repented for the remission of sins, after which they laid their hands upon them that they might receive the Holy Spirit.

Mighty miracles were wrought by them, and also by many of the church. The Nephites and Lamanites were all converted unto the Lord, both in South and North America. And they dwelt in righteousness above three hundred years, but towards the close of the fourth century of the Christian era, they had so far apostatized from God that he suffered great judgments to fall upon them. The Lamanites, at that time, dwelt in South America, and the Nephites in North America.

A great and terrible war commenced between them, which lasted for many years and resulted in the complete overthrow and destruction of the Nephites. This war commenced at the Isthmus of Darien, and was very destructive to both nations for many years. At length, the Nephites were driven before their enemies, a great distance to the north and north-east, and having gathered their whole nation together, both men, women and children, they encamped on and round about the hill Cumorah, where they records were found, which is in the State of New York, about two hundred miles to the west of the city of Albany. Here they were met by the numerous hosts of the Lamanites, and were slain and hewn down and slaughtered, both male and female -- the aged, middle aged, and children.

Hundreds of thousands were slain on both sides, and the nation of the Nephites were destroyed excepting a few who had deserted over to the Lamanites, and a few who escaped into the south country, and a few who fell wounded and were left by the Lamanites on the field of battle for dead, among whom were Mormon and his son Moroni, who were righteous men.

Mormon had made an abridgment from the records of his forefathers, upon plates, which abridgment he entitled the "Book of Mormon", and (being commanded of God) he hid up in the hill Cumorah all the sacred records of his forefathers which were in his possession, except the abridgement called the "Book of Mormon", which he gave to his son Moroni to finish.

Moroni survived his nation a few years, and continued the writings, in which he informs us that the Lamanites hunted those few Nephites who escaped the great and tremendous battle of Cumorah, until they were all destroyed, excepting those who were mingled with the Lamanites. And that he was left alone and kept himself his, for they sought to destroy every Nephite who would not deny the Christ. He furthermore states that the Lamanites were at war one with another, and that the whole face of the land was one continual scene of murdering, robbing, and plundering. He continued the history until the four hundred and twentieth year of the Christian era, which (by commandment of God) he his up the records in the hill Cumorah, where they remained concealed until by the ministry of an angel they were discovered to Mr. Smith, who by the gift and power of God, translated them into the English language by means of the Urim and Thummim, as stated in the foregoing.

PART IV:
THREE WITNESSES

After the book was translated, the Lord raised up witnesses to bear testimony, which reads as follows:

TESTIMONY OF THREE WITNESSES

"Be it known unto all nations, kindreds, tongues, and people, unto whom this work shall come, that we, through the grace of God the Father and our Lord Jesus Christ, have seen the plates which contain this record, which is a record of the people of Nephi, and also of the Lamanites, their brethren, and also of the people of Jared, who came from the tower of which hath been spoken; and we also know that they have been translated by the gift and power of God, for his voice hath declared it unto us; wherefore we know of a surety that the work is true. And we also testify that we have seen the engravings which are upon the plates, and they have been shown unto us by the power of God, and not of man. And we declare with words of soberness that an angel of God cam down from heaven and he brought and laid before our eyes, that we beheld and saw the plates, and the engravings thereon; and we know that it is by the grace of God the Father, and our Lord Jesus Christ, that we beheld and bear record that these things are true; and it is marvelous in our eyes, nevertheless, the voice of the Lord commanded us that we should bear record of it; wherefore, to be obedient unto the commandments of God, we bear testimony of these things. And we know that if we are faithful in Christ, we shal rid our garments of the blood of all men, and be found spotless before the judgment seat of Christ, and shall dwell with him eternally in the heavens. And the honour be to the Father, and to the Son, and to the Holy Ghost, which is one God. Amen."

OLIVER COWDERY
DAVID WHITMER
MARTIN HARRIS

AND ALSO THE TESTIMONY OF EIGHT WITNESSES

"Be it known unto all nations, kindreds, tongues, and people unto whom this work shall come, that Joseph Smith, Jr., the translator of this work, has shown unto us the plates of which hath been spoken, which have the appearance of gold; and as many of the leaves as the said Smith has translated, we did handle with our hands: and we also saw the engravings thereon, all of which has the appearance of ancient work, and of curious workmanship. And this we bear record with words of soberness, that the said Smith has shown unto us, for we have seen and hefted, and now of a surety, that the said Smith has got the plates of which we have spoken. And we give our names unto the world, to witness unto the world that which we have seen; and we lie not, God bearing witness of it.

CHRISTIAN WHITMER
JACOB WHITMER
PETER WHITMER, Jr.
JOHN WHITMER
HIRAM PAGE
JOSEPH SMITH, Sen.
HYRUM SMITH
SAMUEL H. SMITH

Also, in the year 1829, Mr. Smith and Mr. Cowdery, having leaned the correct mode of baptism, from the teachings of the Savior to the ancient Nephites, as recorded in the "Book of Mormon", had a desire to be baptized. But knowing that no one had authority to administer that sacred ordinance in any denomination, they were at a loss to know how the authority was to be restored, and while calling upon the Lord with a desire to be informed on the subject, a holy angel appeared and stood before them, and laid his hands upon their heads, and ordained them, and commanded them to baptize each other, which they accordingly did.

In the year 1830, a large edition of the "Book of Mormon" first appeared in print. And as some began to peruse its sacred pages, the spirit of the Lord bore record to them that it was true. And they were were obedient to its requirements, by coming forth, humbly repenting before the Lord, and being immersed in water for the remission of sins, after which, by commandment of God, hands were laid upon them in the name of the Lord for the gift of the Holy Spirit.

And on the sixth of April, in the year of our Lord one thousand eight hundred and thirty, the "Church of Jesus Christ of Latter Day Saints" was organized, in the town of Manchester, Ontario County, State of New York, North America.

Some few were called and ordained by the spirit of revelation and prophecy, and began to preach and bear testimony, as the spirit gave them utterance; and although they were the weak things of the earth, yet they were strengthened by the Hold Ghost, and gave forth their testimony in great power, by which means many were brought to repentance, and came forward with broken hearts and contrite spirits, and were immersed in water confessing their sins, and were filled with the Holy Ghost by the laying on of hands; and saw visions and prophesied.

Devils were cast out, and the sick were healed by the prayer of faith, and laying on of hands. Thus was the word confirmed unto the faithful by signs following. Thus the Lord raised up witnesses to bear testimony of his name, and lay the foundation of his kingdom in the last days. And thus the hearts of the saints were comforted, and filled with great joy.

In the foregoing, we have related the most important facts concerning the visions and ministry of the angel to Mr. Smith, the discovery of the records, their translation into the English language, and the witnesses raised up to bear testimony of the same.

We have also stated when, and by whom, they were written. That they contain the history of nearly one-half of the globe, from the earliest ages after the flood, until the beginning of the fifth century of the Christian era; that this history is interspersed with many important prophecies, which unfold the great events of the last days, and that in it also is recorded the gospel in its fullness and plainness, as it was revealed by the personal ministry of Christ to the ancient Nephites. We have also given an account of the restoration of the authority in these days, to administer in the ordinances of the gospel; and of the time of the organization of the church; and of the blessings poured out upon the same while yet in its infancy.

PART V:
CHURCH DOCTRINE

We now proceed to give a sketch of the faith and doctrine of this Church.

First, We believe in God the Eternal Father, and in his Son Jesus Christ, and in the Holy Ghost, who bears record of them, the same throughout all ages and for ever.

We believe that all mankind, by the transgression of their first parents and not by their own sins, were brought under the curse and penalty of that transgression which consigned them to an eternal banishment from the presence of God, and their bodies to an endless sleep in the dust never more to rise, and their spirits to endless misery under the power of Satan; and that, in this awful condition, they were utterly lost and fallen, and had no power of their own to extricate themselves therefrom.

We believe that through the sufferings, death, and atonement of Jesus Christ all mankind, without one exception, are to be completely and fully redeemed, both body and spirit, from the endless banishment and curse, to which they were consigned, by Adam's transgression; and that this universal salvation and redemption of the whole human family from the endless penalty of the original sin, is effected, without any conditions whatsoever on their part; that is, that they are not required to believe, or repent, or be baptized, or do any thing else, in order to be redeemed from that penalty: for whether they believe or disbelieve, whether they repent or remain impenitent, whether they are baptized or unbaptized, whether they keep the commandments or break them, whether they are righteous or unrighteous, it will make no difference in relation to their redemption, both soul and body, from the penalty of Adam's transgression. The most righteous man that ever lived on the earth, and the most wicked wretch of the whole human family, were both placed under the same curse, without any transgression or agency of their own, and they both, alike, will be redeemed from that curse, without any agency or conditions on their part. Paul says, Rom. V. 18 "Therefore as by the offense of one, judgment came upon ALL men to condemnation; even so, by the righteousness of one, the free gift came upon ALL men unto the justification of life." This is the reason why ALL men are redeemed from the grave. This is the reason that the spirits of ALL men are restored to their bodies. This is the reason that ALL men are redeemed from their first banishment, and restored into the presence of God, and this is the reason that the Saviour said, John xii 32 "If I be lifted up from the earth I will draw ALL men unto me." After this full, complete, and universal redemption, restoration, and salvation of the whole of Adam's race, through the atonement of Jesus Christ, without faith, repentance, baptism, or any other works, then, all and every one of them, will enjoy eternal life and happiness, never more to be banished from the presence of God, IF they themselves have committed no sin: for the penalty of the original sin can have no more power over them at all, for Jesus hath destroyed its power and broken the bands of the first death, and obtained the victory over the grave, and delivered all its captives, and restored them from their first banishment into the presence of his Father; hence eternal life will then be theirs; IF they themselves are not found transgressors of some law.

We believe that all mankind, in their infant state, are incapable of knowing good and evil, and of obeying or disobeying a law, and that, therefore, there is no law given to them, and that where there is no law, there is no transgression; hence they are innocent, and if they should all die in their infant state, they would enjoy eternal life, not being transgressors themselves, neither accountable for Adam's sin.

We believe that all mankind, in consequence of the fall, after they grow up from their infant state, and come to the years of understanding, know good and evil, and are capable of obeying or disobeying a law, and that a law is given against doing evil, and that the penalty affixed is a second banishment from the presence of God, both body and spirit, after they have been redeemed from the FIRST banishment and band restored into his presence.

We believe, that the penalty of this second law can have no effect upon persons who have not had the privilege, in this life, of becoming acquainted therewith; for although the light that is in them, teaches them good and evil, yet that light does not teach them the law against doing evil, nor the penalty thereof. And although they have done things worthy of many stripes, yet the law cannot be brought to bear against them, and its penalty be inflicted, because they can plead ignorance thereof. Therefore they will be judged, not by the revealed law which they have been ignorant of, but by the law of their conscience, the penalty thereof being a few stripes.

We believe that all who have done evil, having a knowledge of the law, or afterwards, in this life, coming to the knowledge thereof, are under its penalty, which is not inflicted in this world; but in the world to come therefore such, in this world, are prisoners, shut up under the sentence of the law, awaiting, with awful fear for the time of judgment, when the penalty shall be inflicted, consigning them to a second banishment from the presence of their Redeemer, who had redeemed them from the penalty of the FIRST law. But, enquires the sinner, is there no way for my escape? Is my case hopeless? Can I not devise some way by which I can extricate myself from the penalty of this SECOND law, and escape this SECOND banishment? The answer is, if thou canst hide thyself from the all-searching eye of an Omnipresent God, that he shall not find thee, or if thou canst prevail with him to deny justice its claim, or if thou canst clothe thyself with power, and contend with the Almighty, and prevent him from executing the sentence of the law, then thou canst escape. If thou canst cause repentance, or baptism in water, or any of thine own works, to atone for the least of thy transgressions, then thou canst deliver thyself from the awful penalty that awaits thee. But, be assured, O sinner, that thou canst not devise any way of thine own to escape, nor do any thing that will atone for thy sins. Therefore, thy case is hopeless, unless God hath devised some way for thy deliverance; but do not let despair seize upon thee: for though thou art under the sentence of a broken law, and hast no power to atone for thy sins, and redeem thyself therefrom, yet there is hope in thy case; for he, who gave the law, has devised a way for thy deliverance. That same Jesus, who hath atoned for the original sin, and will redeem all mankind from the penalty thereof, hath also atoned for thy sins, and offereth salvation and deliverance to thee, on certain conditions to be complied with on thy part

We believe that the first condition to be complied with on the part of sinners is, to believe in God, and in the sufferings and death of his Son Jesus Christ, to atone for the sins of the whole world, and in his resurrection and ascension on high, to appear in the presence of his Father, to make intercessions for the children of men, and in the Holy Ghost, which is given to all who obey the gospel.

That the second condition is, to repent, that is, all who believe, according to the first condition, are required to come humbly before God, and confess their sins with a broken heart and contrite spirit, and to turn away from them, and cease from all their evil deeds, and make restitution to all they have in any way injured, as far as it is in their power.

That the third condition is, to be baptized by immersion in water, in the name of the Father, Son, and Holy Ghost, for remission of sins; and that this ordinance is to be administered by one who is called and authorized of Jesus Christ to baptize, otherwise it is illegal, and of no advantage, and not accepted by him; and that it is to be administered only to those persons, who believe and repent, according to the two preceding conditions.

And that the fourth condition is, to receive the laying on of hands, in the name of Jesus Christ, for the gift of the Holy Ghost; and that this ordinance is to be administered by the apostles or elders, whom the lord Jesus hath called and authorized to lay on hands, otherwise it is of no advantage, being illegal in the sight of God; and that it is to be administered only to those persons, who believe, repent, and are baptized into this church, according to the three preceding conditions. These are the first conditions of the gospel. All who comply with them receive forgiveness of sins, and are made partakers of the Holy Ghost. Through these conditions, they become the adopted sons and daughters of God. Through this process, they are born, again first of water, and then of the spirit, and become children of the kingdom—heirs of God—saints of the most High—the church of the first born—the elect people, and heirs to a celestial inheritance, eternal in the presence of God. After complying with these principles, their names are enrolled in the book of the names of the righteous.

They are then required to be humble, to be meek and lowly in heart, to watch and pray, to deal justly; and inasmuch as they have the niches riches of this world, to feed the hungry and clothe the naked, according to the dictates of wisdom and prudence; to comfort the afflicted, to bind up the broken-hearted, and to do all the good that is in their power: and besides all these things, they are required to meet together as often as circumstances will admit, and partake of bread and wine, in remembrance of the broken body and shed blood of the lord Jesus; and, in short, to continue faithful to the end, in all the duties enjoined upon them by the word and spirit of Christ. "It is the duty and privilege of the saints thus organized upon the everlasting gospel, to believe in and enjoy all the gifts, powers, and blessings which flow from the Holy Spirit. Such, for instance, as the gifts of revelation, Prophecy, visions, the ministry of angels, healing the sick by the laying on of hands in the name of Jesus, the working of miracles, and, in short, all the gifts as mentioned in Scripture, or as enjoyed by the ancient saints." We believe that inspired apostles and prophets, together with all the officers as mentioned in the New Testament, are necessary to be in the Church in these days.

We believe that there has been a general and awful apostacy from the religion of the New Testament, so that all the known world have been left for centuries without the church of Christ among them; without a priesthood authorized of God to administer ordinances; that every one of the churches has perverted the gospel; some in one way, and some in another. For instance, almost every church has done away "immersion for remission of sins." Those few who have practiced practised it for remission of sins, have done away the ordinance of the "laying on of hands" upon baptized believers for the gift of the Holy Ghost. Again, the few who have practised practiced this last ordinance, have perverted the first, or have done away the ancient gifts, and powers, and blessings, which flow from the Holy Spirit, or have said to inspired apostles and prophets, we have no need of you in the body in these days. Those few, again, who have believed in, and contended for the miraculous gifts and powers of the Holy Spirit, have perverted the ordinances, or done them away. Thus all the churches preach false doctrines, and pervert the gospel, and instead of having authority from God to administer its ordinances, they are under the curse of God for perverting it. Paul says, Gal. i. 8, "Though we, or an angel from heaven, preach any other gospel unto you than that which we have preached unto you, let him be accursed."

We believe that there are a few, sincere, honest, and humble persons, who are striving to do according to the best their understanding; but, in many respects, they err in doctrine, because of false teachers and the precepts of men, and that they will receive the fulness of the gospel with gladness, as soon as they hear it.

The gospel in the "Book of Mormon," is the same as that in the New Testament, and is revealed in great plainness, so that no one that reads it can misunderstand its principles. It has been revealed by the angel, to be preached as a witness to all nations, first to the Gentiles, and then to the Jews, then cometh the downfall of Babylon. Thus fulfilling the vision of John, which he beheld on the isle of Patmos, Rev. xiv. 6, 7, 8 "And I saw," says John, "another angel fly in the midst of heaven, having the everlasting gospel to preach unto them that dwell on the earth, and to every nation, and kindred, and tongue, and people, saying, with a loud voice, Fear God, and give glory to him, for the hour of his judgment is come: and worship him that made heaven, and earth, and the sea, and the fountains of waters. And there followed another angel, saying,

Babylon is fallen, is fallen, that great city, because she made all nations drink of the wine of the wrath of her fornication."

Many revelations and prophecies have been given to this church since its rise, which have been printed and sent forth to the world. These also contain the gospel in great plainness, and instructions of infinite importance to the saints. They also unfold the great events that await this generation; the terrible judgments to be poured forth upon the wicked, and the blessings and glories to be given to the righteous. We believe that God will continue to give revelations by visions, by the ministry of angels, and by the inspiration of the Holy Ghost, until the saints are guided unto all truth, that is, until they come in possession of all the truth there is in existence, and are made perfect in knowledge. So long, therefore, as they are ignorant of any thing past, present, or to come, so long, we believe, they will enjoy the gift of revelation. And when in their immortal and perfect state—when they enjoy "the measure of the stature of the fulness of Christ"— when they are made perfect in one, and become like their Saviour, then they will be in possession of all knowledge, wisdom, and intelligence: then all things will be theirs, whether [pr]incipalities or powers, thrones or dominions; and i[n] short, then they will be filled with all the fulness of God. And what more can they learn? What more can they know? What more can they enjoy? Then they will no longer need revelation.

We believe that wherever the people enjoy the religion of the New Testament, there they enjoy visions, revelations, the ministry of angels, &c. And that wherever these blessings cease to be enjoyed, there they also cease to enjoy the religion of the New Testament.

We believe that God has raised up this church, in order to prepare a people for his second coming in the clouds of heaven, in power, and great glory; and that then the saints who are asleep in their graves will be raised, and reign with him on earth a thousand years.

And we now bear testimony to all, both small and great, that the Lord of Hosts hath sent us with a message of glad tidings—the everlasting gospel, to cry repentance to the nations, and prepare the way of his second coming. Therefore repent O ye nations, both Gentiles and Jews, and cease from all your evil deeds, and come forth with broken hearts and contrite spirits, and be baptized in water, in the name of the Father, Son and Holy Ghost, for remission of sins, and ye shall receive the gift of the Holy Spirit, by the laying on of the hands of the Apostles or Elders of this church; and signs shall follow them that believe, and if they continue faithful to the end, they shall be saved. But woe unto them, who hearken not to the message which God has now sent, for the day of vengeance and burning is at hand, and they shall not escape. Therefore REMEMBER, O reader and perish not!

www.ingramcontent.com/pod-product-compliance
Lightning Source LLC
LaVergne TN
LVHW041501070426
835507LV00009B/735